Scholastic Phonics

Real-life Monsters

Published in the UK by Scholastic Education, 2023
Scholastic Distribution Centre, Bosworth Avenue, Tournament Fields, Warwick, CV34 6UQ
Scholastic Ireland, 89E Lagan Road, Dublin Industrial Estate, Glasnevin, Dublin, D11 HP5F

SCHOLASTIC and associated logos are trademarks and/or registered trademarks of Scholastic Inc.
www.scholastic.co.uk
© 2023 Scholastic
1 2 3 4 5 6 7 8 9   3 4 5 6 7 8 9 0 1 2

Printed by Ashford Colour Press
The book is made of materials from well-managed, FSC®-certified forests and other controlled sources.

A CIP catalogue record for this book is available from the British Library.
ISBN 978-0702-32105-4

All rights reserved. This book is sold subject to the condition that it shall not, by way of trade or otherwise, be lent, hired out or otherwise circulated in any form of binding or cover other than that in which it is published. No part of this publication may be reproduced, stored in a retrieval system, or transmitted in any form or by any other means (electronic, mechanical, photocopying, recording or otherwise) without prior written permission of Scholastic.

Every effort has been made to trace copyright holders for the works reproduced in this publication, and the publishers apologise for any inadvertent omissions.

Author
Suzy Ditchburn

Editorial team
Rachel Morgan, Vicki Yates, Caroline Hale, Jennie Clifford

Design team
Dipa Mistry, Andrea Lewis, We Are Grace

Photographs
Cover Philip Thurston/iStock
p1, 6 guenterguni/iStock
p7 LoweStock/iStock
p4, 8 AYImages/iStock
p9 Sergey Uryadnikov/Shutterstock
p10–11, 24 Luis Montero de Espinosa/Shutterstock
p11 reptiles4all/iStock
p12 Kishore Dharuman/iStock
p4, 13 Skynavin/Shutterstock
p4, 14 Gunther Fraulob/iStock
p15 Sean Nel/Shutterstock
p16, 24 Ramon Carretero/Shutterstock
p4, 17 Ryan Cake/iStock
p3, 18–19 crisod/iStock
p20 VDCM image/iStock
p4, 21 Ken Griffiths/Shutterstock
p22 scubaluna/iStock
p23 guenterguni/iStock

Help your child to read!

This book practises these letters and letter sounds.
Point and say the sounds with your child:

- o (as in 'cobra')
- i (as in 'spider')
- a (as in 'mako')
- e (as in 'be')
- a–e (as in 'snakes')
- i–e (as in 'bite')
- e–e (as in 'these')
- ie (as in 'bodies')

Your child may need help to read these common tricky words:

- some
- of
- are
- they
- little
- you
- the
- have
- to
- when
- their
- one
- all
- full
- there

Before reading

- Look at the cover picture and read the title together. Read the back cover blurb to your child.
- Ask your child: *Have you ever been scared of an animal? Which one and why?*
- Talk about the image in the magnifying glass.

During reading

- If your child gets stuck on a word, remind them to sound it out and then blend the sounds to read the word: s-p-i-d-er, spider.
- If they are still stuck, show them how to read the word.
- Enjoy looking at the pictures together. Pause to talk about the information.

After reading

- Talk about the images on page 24. What can your child tell you about them?
- Ask your child: *Which animal did you find the most fearsome?*
- Talk with your child about which animal you would like to learn more about. What did they find most interesting about it?

Some of these are seen as real-life monsters.

They can be big and intimidating or little with a jumbo bite.

You might find some of these alarming.

The biggest lizard on the planet is the Komodo dragon.

They have hard scales and claws to defend.

When they bite their enemies with their big jaws, they poison them.

They can eat a goat in one go!

These snakes have scales that are jagged so they are named saw-scaled vipers.

They are quick to strike their enemies. Their venom can kill a human.

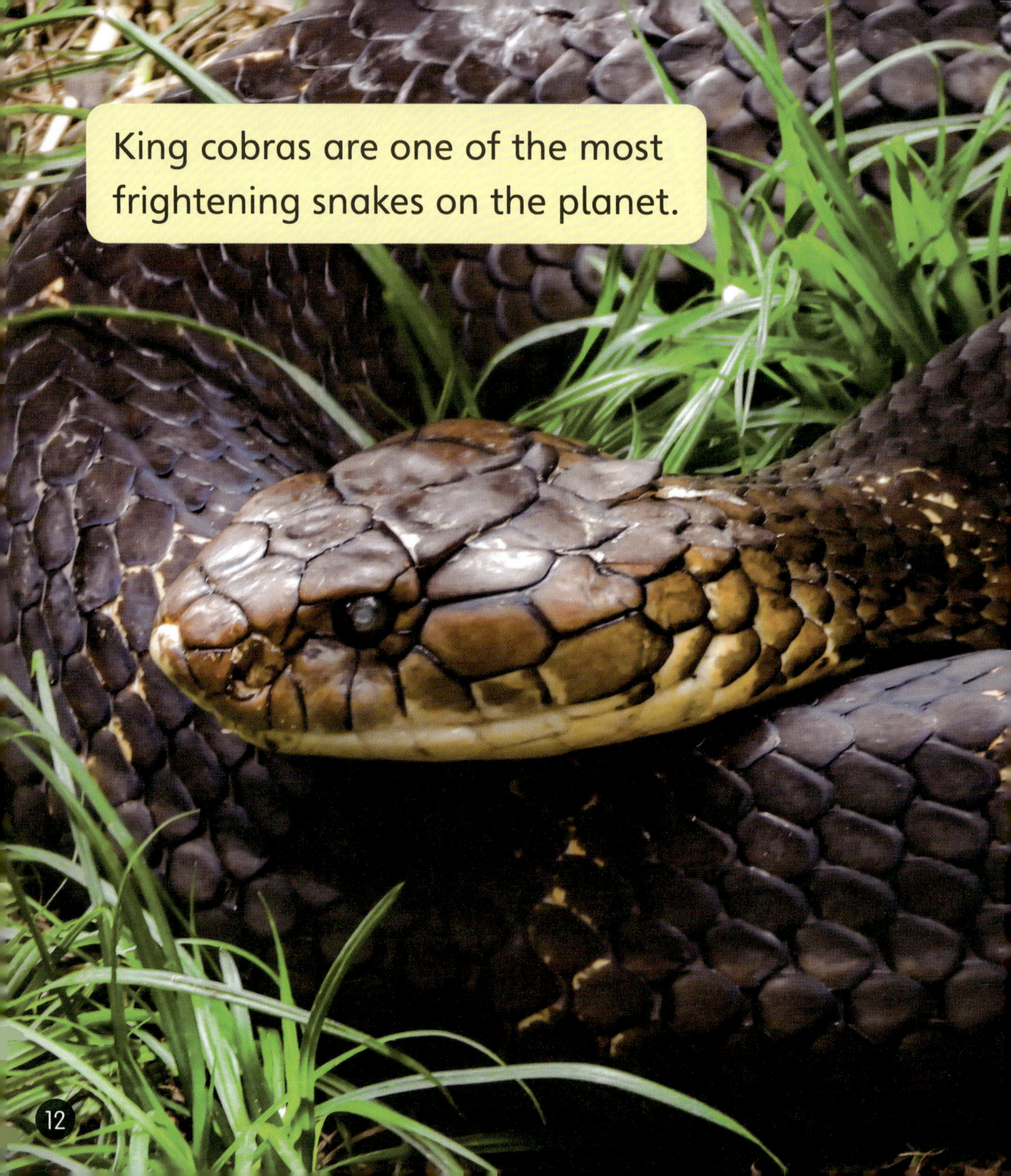

King cobras are one of the most frightening snakes on the planet.

Their bodies can lift up to attack their enemies.

Lions can be intimidating. The male lions oversee the pride.

The female lions hunt for food. They hunt at night to surprise their target.

Sharks are some of the most feared fish in the sea. They can hunt for a meal even in the dark.

The mako shark has the strongest bite of all sharks.

Lionfish don't look intimidating, but their spines contain poison.

spines

They have few predators thanks to these spines, and their stripes help them to hide.

Spiders are little, but some can still be frightening.

The funnel-web spider presents the most risk to humans. Its bite is full of venom.

The good news is that there is treatment for spider venom these days.

All these real-life monsters may be frightening – but they attack to survive, so just stay away!

Talk about it!